Shattered Illusions

Jeremy Void

Other books by Jeremy Void

Fiction

Derelict America

Nefarious Endeavors

Sex Drugs & Violence: Incomplete Stories for the Incomplete Human

Nonfiction

My Story: The Short Version

Chaos Writing

Postal Prose: The Musings of a Tortured Soul, For Sure

Poetry

Smash a Lightbulb: Poetry for Lowlifes

Just a Kid

The Lost Letters

An Art Form: The Crass Poetry Collection

The TR*TH

My Psychedelic Suicide

A Crime of Passion

Anti-Matter: Poems for the Manic Nihilist

The SkullFuck Collection

Erase Your Face

I Need Help

A Crass Philosophy

Pre-Apocalyptic

Breaking News

Spoken word albums by Jeremy Void

available at www.bandcamp.jeremyvoid.com

Absurd Nihilism

Word Vomit

Irrelevant Discourse

Shattered Illusions

Jeremy Void

Shattered Illusions

ISBN Number:
978-0-578-19150-8

dedication

Contents

My Psychedelic Suicide

1.

the demonic symbiotic spine
threaded thru your mind,
twisting & retching as it
reaches into the sky
has got me lost in a whirlwind of lies
poking thru my eye
making me cry unfortunate tears
that wisp down my back
treading electric webbing
kinetic & spherical
a swirling of emotions going
up into me like spicy blades
of sonic might---of ultra-disarray that
wraps its ultra-sonic rays all the way around
my head. blistering & vicious
it hits me w/ a kick strong enough
to lift the plates that carry the earth
in a sort of cocoon---a blue-&-green ball
that bounces as if made
of rubbery film, bubbling over
explosive to the point of imploding.
im lucid & destructive
a mix of black-&-white force
that bleeds gray all over the city streets.
im lost in an ambient spin
lost in a patriotic backfire
the shit is coming back up &
spilling all over the central nervous system.

2.

the owl sits up on its perch
watching me thru foggy eyes.
the hawk dies & flops on the ground
as bats frolic amid the death & the
owl hoots & sneers in mock unisons to
the mayhem. a fox pokes its head out
of the whales stomach, w/ a foamy grimace
on its face.
its sick so sick.
its sad so sad.
the whale mutates & grows
to the weight of the woods
around it, bright & big
epically sieging & destructively
sound as everything breaks down
around it/

im walking thru the forest
listening to the sounds:
the branches crunching
the leaves rustling beneath
my feet---stomp stomp stomp.
clomp! goes the eagle searching.
the wind blows & barrels.
the egg hatches & out
comes a pterodactyl cawing & flapping;

it wraps its wings around the earth
pulling it in & off it surges from
its perch in the leaves >>>>
CAAAAAAW

hell rises.
the sky falls >>>
crashing   smashing
fanning out as the animals live
lividly & sinfully devoted
to destruction.

i listen, standing on
the edge, at the beginning, in
the cave i stand on the epochs
awaiting change, & something breaks
inside me.
CAAAAAAW! says the pterodactyl, a devil
lish beast reaching its wings &
casting a diabolical scheme of maddening
breaches; the world is beached

BEACHED
BEACHED
BEACHED
BEACHED

i shut down.
my mind falls apart.
i sit up.
my head drops & hits
the concrete w/ a plop/
the beast is in
the beast wins my right
& i wonder why

i let it....

the heavens come to life.
the angels flap & strive.
the world beneath me
swirls deeply in the sacrilegious
manner its known to roll
w/.

the riot begins here.
the angels come down.
the hawk is riveting & bright.
the bats are free for strife.
your world melts
whereas mine grows stronger & harder
sound enough to withstand your
wrathful ways---hahahahahahaha!

i live in the sky.
i live in the mind.
the whys have told me lies
& I wonder what brought me
here
this
madness/

surfs up, dude!

the waves roll past hell while
the demons laugh so hard
they fall even harder & the angels
are up there shooting arrows from
their flaming bows which morph into
snakes that take a bite outta crime.

i live in the sky.
your mind is mine.
i wonder why this is life
but it is
it is

it is ...

becuz i sed so....

the fire ignites
pacifies/
the oceans are a bright blue
as the boats slue on the surface
of the abyss like eels
rolling   like snakes, & the boots
are coming down & crashing into my my my
fuckin suicide.

3.

the sky breathes
harsh hypnotic breaths
seeping outta the systematic
tornado. the air gets tighter
wrapping me in its tendrils
dripping w/ sweaty morphine.
im up in the clouds running for my life
my deadly sins speeding up
behind me
riotous & absurdly thunderous
apeshit raisins.

i sit in the sky, rain falling all around me.
i sit in the clouds, thunder & lightning
ricocheting off the blue beyond
& i am in space.

i go to sleep
but the sound of riotous tears hits & i awaken/
im sitting on my face
as my nose bleeds, succumbing to fear.
my ears throb, succumbing to soundless
might & riotous cucumbers;
they wrap their plummeting ancestors
around me & lift me till
im plunging into the sky

rising to the ground, the whole wide world
rammingly vivid in its visceral sense.
my whole life i waited for this.
the money comes to me when
i go to sleep at night. the world feels like
a bee sting when i live to
sloooooooooooow for this apeshit reality you will
find me in when i run w/
motorcycles cutting a path thru the ice
rink.

the edge of the madness
pulsates in beauty, so horrifying
& delightful i rip out my own eyes.
the sound is like an eardrum
bashed w/ bolts of lightning
stinging me & sending me
to planet neutron.

the air rattles & shakes
me, whipping me & breaking me
to the point of imploding & i sit in
the impotent beetle as pliers press
me trying to pull me back out....

they can try.

but the beetle skitters on the
hardwood floor amid strikes
& flashes of thunder, amid
the pounding of lightnings biting
pressure as it roils & claws
& tinfoil surrounds me hardly
ever able to rip apart but i can try ...

& so i try.

i try to match the mighty pull.
i try to match the mighty rolling
of 2 tons of force coming down
on me harder than hard, than you
as your fat explodes & blubber plows me from
every direction, sent & disordered
mowing me down....

ill mow you down.
ill mow you down.
ill mow into you plowing
& disastrously destructive......

gonna zap you, dude///

gonna wrap you
like eminem wraps peanut butter
w/ bread.
the music is hard & i wonder
why it barks so crowded w/ feces///
....loudly & hardly are one & the same.
the soundlessness crowds me on the subway
when i stand tall in the clouds
& watch as the whole earth
melts into jelly.
the jelly undulates beneath Gods foot.

his spikey toenails.

4.

silence---it roars
bright & loud & vicious
it soars---thru clouds
& overseas & down
in the valley it billows
& blunders, the thunderous thrashing
the lights are flashing, strikes of
lightning---& the sounds fade
dissipate blank & jaded.
the world---going retro
people infest it like children in
a playground running & fighting
biting its a rumble.
the silence the wonder the world
it goes underground drops off
as a new sound rises a pounding
a rasping
fierce & electronic
it feasts eating things that
fall away & fade into
oblivion------
the lights go out
the silence rumbles up
& out surfaces as the ground
undulates in epileptic strokes.
i speak i spoke---the people

are stoked they crawl & croak
reaching & retching arms spreading
rapidly wondering   thundering.
the silence speaks
feeds
wreaks havoc on the seers
the believers.
twisted churning & burning me up
into oblivion...

5.

the city sleeps....
i walk the streets alone,
feeling grim & bold
feeling alive & whole
feeling like a demon & the whole
entire world
belongs to me.

the moon paves
a translucent path
straight thru the clouds,
a spotlight in the night, bright with
terror & glee it makes me shiver
quiver
a sliver & a dip & a drop
i feel so bad ...
bad to my liver
& i think im getting bigger.

i creep around the corner & the slight
cool makes me feel hot
makes me feel fearless & ready for
adventure---me & my music rising up
& immersing me with fast, melodic sounds.

its an ugly night,

but i love it.
its a frightful delight
that brings me cheers
& i cant let that down

not now
not then
not yesterday or tomorrow
cuz the now is delightfully sound
wrapping me up in barbed wire
lifting me off my feet & spinning me around
& around
& around

i feel for the night
& it feels for me.
i feel it pulsating in my veins
we are one & the same.

the night & i are out tonight
& we wont be stopped
bargained with
or bought
cuz theres only one thing
that we want------------

a nightly adventure
with a nightly tune to overlay it all
& then ill go home

& ill never sleep again.

6.

immersed in flies
the music like a shrine
a distraction from the invasion of flies.
i sit in the ill apartment, in the
hustle the bustle the flux of filth arising
& i think im dying ...
the world like wax, the sun like
flames of volley & its coming
down on me fast.
the music fading & my mind ablaze
with disharmony, fazing in & out &
in & out, too quick like a siege of
waves roiling in the sea, gaining size
strengthening & brightening &
disintegrating like the devils nectar//
distraught, in a world not of my own
in another world a world big & fat
growing outta proportion as it kicks your ass.
the flies crawl on the waste
crowding the garbage like vermin.
its sick & makes me sick.
i needa fog the place, a billowing, gray smoke
growing outta the nozzle.
toxic & killer, it kills & destroys the flies.
i sit in the midst of the buzzing swarm
the flies clinging to discarded soda cans

empty coffee mugs im in such a jam.
the trash is overflowing.
the ground is covered with paper & trash.
cleanliness cant be found here as
i huddle in this wasted life dissipating
fazing in & out & in & out, & spiraling
spiraling
spiraling
spiraling around my head im dizzy from the sickening
mess that covers every square inch---cant get
the dishes becuz if I try
the flies will billow up & swarm me
get in my nose
my mouth
my ears its so freaking gross.

what am i to do?

7.

in a labyrinth the size of my head
the doctors search for meaning
they search for purpose
they search for reason, but they cant find their way
out///
its just too complex.

in a labyrinth the size of my head
many good men get lost, men with
high degrees following the paths that my brain
shapes & forms & spins around
& around
& around, but they cant find their way
out///
its just too complex.

in a labyrinth the size of my head
thoughts mow thru the lanes like ghosts
evading the doctors, the psychiatrists,
cuz you cant psycho-analyze me
you cant put me under the microscope
cuz the things that make me tick are
the things that make me tick & in this maze
youll find that they arent very sane....
they bite & they stab & they sting.
the doctors curse.

the doctors search
& search
& search, but they cant find their way
out///
its just too complex.

ive devised a labyrinth, spun a web
of thoughts, so devious & perverse, something
for the doctors to converse about, something
for them to say about me
something something something
something, but i cant find my way
out///
its just too complex.

8.

solitude---4 walls
plain
insane
lacking anything
to which i can relate....
the padded walls of a dream/
i bounce from wall to wall
my straightjacket tight &
holding me in

i sit on the edge of madness
            on the epoch of
            paranoia---these voices
following me down the road.
i hear things---& this
makes me crazy?---im really just
lazy
my life in a haze. i bathe in
blood dont make me madd
just sad
so sad ...
sad sad sad
im bad   really really bad.

sounds   coming at me
from all sides they bite

they rip
they nip at my skin---yip yip yip.........................

im running
times running out
the clouds overhead
smother me lock me in---------im
stuck treading guts of a dream....
its only a dream i say.
its just a dream i repeat.
i shout i scream. i stomp my feet
on the bone layered floor
beneath me.
the dungeon holds me in
the doors are jammed & i slam
bam bam thank you maam
i ram into them they creak.
the floor morphs & im floating
the river flowing beneath me.
i walk on water
or air
the whirlwind is swirling
& lifting me up---& I go up up up
flipping flying crying
the whole world explodes
& i feel low
the bombs blow holes
in my head my mind.

im wasted now
dilapidated
so goddamn agitated.

its only a dream i say.
its just a dream i repeat.

they lock me in a hole

away from reality, & i
beat the bars bang the bars
thwack them hard.
my knuckles char
break apart
i sit on the dungeons floor
weeping
peeing
& then i bend
& spew------& i know im
       done for....

9.

i wake up.
i sit up.
my head aches.
my body melts.
my mind dissipates
as the brain undulates
& my legs break crack crunch
& bunch together & i trip & go down
straight down------ouch!

10.

in a trance:
i see stars....
i see the sun
i see you & what you are
& i cant stand for it
any longer,
so i kick over tables & chairs
i have a fit i throw a brick
i break the television set---who needs it?
anyway

in a trance:
i see the world for what it is
for the first time ever.
for the first time ever i rise above it
above the madness that ricochets off walls
& the floor double-crosses & i stop stop stop
stoppit! but it comes back up & spins around me
the spin quick & limber whipping me off my feet
& i flop   drop   clomp   plop---it hits me hard
on the head....
you think id be dead.
youd think so but
im coming back forya....

11.

the world unfolds around me
the worlds mold into something more
it snaps & whips & quick-steps around me
all the way to babylon & im alive
the pimps & the whores pass me by
& im alive
i ride my skateboard thru babylon city.
everyone stares at me like
im some kinda freak.
like im the freak?
this is babylon, home of the freaks
creeps
& cretins crawling up the walls as they conspire
to pounce....
& im the freak?
look at me riding my skateboard
thru downtown hell, the fires rippling past me
high tides trilling up & up & up
up up up---higher than the sky
im alive, an eyeball follows me as i ride the board
it watches me as i flee
up the street.

crowds suddenly coming at me like a wall
i hit them head-on & take a sudden
dive into the bustle the riffraff stirring a storm

of a thing as i go splat on the moon.
soon i will understand but for now
its lost on me & im lost in space.
this gleeful bee has got me pinned to
the ground, it laughs & mocks & jokes
& hawks a ludicrous loogy in my face.
the wad of grossness splatters in my eye
i try to push myself up but the laughing bee
is too strong & holds me there as more bees
flock the happy one & say let go of em mannnn.
let go of em, leave em be---no pun intended, says
one hairy one as it rises & fires a dart that
clips the gleeful one
& pins him to a tree------& im up
& running, running for the hills, the hills growing
as i come closer & closer, the sandy plains
wobbling beneath my quick-moving feet, hitching
kicking
pushing & jabbing
ramming one foot after another, &
im swept up by a crazy blast of wind pulling me
straight up & releasing me as i sail the skies my shirt
fanning out to create a cape as i soar the 7
skies the sun bright & warm & it winks at me.
the bees are on my tail & now another crazy blast
of wind pushes into me & i wobble wobble wobble
my shirt rips & im falling, flailing, plunging to
---------------to my horrible
ridiculous
somewhat ironic
demise that with a jolting pressure surges up &
meets me halfway there---the ground breaks
my fall, my collision breaks my legs, & my face plunges
into the pavement & I crack three teeth my way down.
i smile all toothless but it was worth it---
thats xtreme sports forya, getting on a skateboard
in the first place signs off on the risks of
a devastating faceplant that leaves me a broken

mess.

i get up & brush myself off
jus to see that babylon hasnt changed
one bit since i was gone.

12.

immersed in darkness
i sit in the pub & listen
to the country tunes
bleating outward & trilling
as the two men onstage
sing harmoniously.
           i wait in the dark\\
           my time
           my day
           has yet to start.

the sharp guitar riff
cutting thru ice
& knocking down glaciers im awake
      i think
im asleep---more likely the case.
a hailstorm of progressive
notes & chords coming to life
slithering deep in the backroom
a quivering shiver trilling
quietly up my spine frightfully
designed to demolish buildings
like a j - j ------ j - j ------ j - j - j - jackhammer
ramming thru steel & concrete
arriving on the other side
of mayhem deep its delicious

      & delightful
a bite a stab a tear a break in the
    fabric wound tight
      around me---gonna create
      chaos as the song pumps
& jabs into me it stings
deeply
sensationally
delighted to know you

i wonder in the dark
as the relentless jam slam-dunks
a ricocheting funklike tumor springing up
from deep down in the sea i wonder------
the song stops & ceases

& thank god for that…………………………………………………………….

The Nameless City* | defaced

1.

Magical the way
clouds sit scattered
among me.
Like I'm in heaven
cruising beneath
the beaming sun
I'm in a plane
          sky-high
the clouds like blossoming flowers
like I'm in the garden of the gods.
Thousands of feet below me
the world rushes past....

2.

The train rumbles
I sit here waiting
      outta money
      outta breath
      my heart ricocheting
in my chest

The darkness pours through
the window like I'm in
a void

The occasional light
shines through
my head aches   I'm so distraught
Mentally I'm
      slamming my fist
      through the glass
      penetrating the void
      becoming one with
      the night

lost in Boston's
finest
        black hole

3.

Lights illuminate
the bank of bricks
        on which I'm perched

Cigarette smoke gushes
through my lips
        drag after drag.

A Wednesday night
            (it feels like a Friday)
I wait
        for the train

The sky etched with
pollution smoke and vile
the city
        people hustle   like sheep
        to the slaughter
lost in the lights a bustle
of vanity   wasted   here

        The stroke of midnight
tick, tick---tock
            unloaded....

4.

On the red line now
       blasted
              by the past
thinking about the time
I tagged Lethal Erection
       in bright red
down by the red line loading dock
at Park Street
       when I slapped the T-driver
       in the face
when drunk cuz
I reached my hand out to graze
the train with the tips of my fingers
       the conductor stuck out his head
       through the open window
          and------*whammo!*

I tell my friend nobody's ever
fucked with me in Rutland
       after
he tells me he's been hassled
a bunch.
           He says
it's because I grew up in Boston
I'm used to the big city
and all its heinous customs

        the rush the bustle and the flow
of trains and traffic jams and
people lined up like cattle
        the fights
            the drugs
                the nights and the thugs
lost in an antagonistic world
        lost ... period

losing myself to waste and decay

a manic mudslide
        rolling
                faster and faster
smashing crashing and bashing through
this side of the world.

Lost ... to myself
        I think I'm wasted again

5.

The power of suggestion
a battle of wits
      who will persevere?
Voices---I'm locked inside
      as though swimming in
      a tub of jello
Voices---I'm stuck in the pull
      a tether of ambitions
      coiling right around my head.

People---they sit on benches
      still as a petrified toad
      waiting to leap out
          but stuck like a fly
          caught in a web

I'm stuck in a backslide
going nowhere
      outta the rut
      into a tub of
      molten lava
sliding down volcanic ashes
         ---I'm shaken and distraught.

Do not utter my name!
      when you go to bed at night....

6.

In a strange room
      blank and deserted
my friend sits at the desk
I sit on the bed
old-school oi! buzzes and rasps
from somewhere far away
a cat brushes up against me
I smoke my cigarette
      taken
      lost
      holding on by
      a rapidly unravelling thread
There is nothing in the world
that beats it.
Sex---no!
Drugs---no!
Cheap pornography masturbation roofied mistresses bondage
    and leather whips and chains cash money blow-up dolls or
    cigarette burns and razor slashes
      nothing adds up to
      THIS

Bliss in bondage
taken hostage
a barbed lozenge
the world under my control

My friend sings along
to the tunes
"We're no angels we're no saints,"
        he sings.

Wednesday night, it feels like a Friday
Nothing to do but
stay awake and drink my coffee.

      He talks but I don't follow.
      I just nod my head and say, "Yeah yeah yeah."

7.

In a dark car, parked by
the ocean
cars zip by in the distance
a real straight-shooter,
a line of powder sniffed
a syringe tapped and a plunger
depressed, the pressure firing
straight through me
I'm alive I'm on fire
my veins pop out of me
like bubble wrap
clattering
   like marbles
  the music comes on
   shattering the endless silence.
A cramped existence

on the edge of dissipation

loosely devoted

widely denownced
  I sip the wine
  it breaks through my skull
    My brain
    My head

                  My mind
it all breaks down
leaving me a wretched waste
of a mutant disease.
So glad to be in the city tonight
cruising with my unruly minion
of 1,000 broken dreams
a menacing façade that cuts the ice
and I'm back where I started
back at the car, and the truck

rumbles down the swirling road
            The time: 2:30 AM
I bite the bucket when the
            diminishing
            twisting
            seesawing
avenue breaks apart
into two different lanes
and we come head to head with

a dead end///

It's a skewed belief
a system of spilt tears
creeping through my fingertips.

I run my hand through my hair.
You run your hands over your breasts.
I see your nipples they shine
like demonic bloodshot eyes
watching me as I cross over the length
of the crusty, established, brooding moon.

A serpent sleeps as the ghouls
roam the streets/

8.

Your pretty eyes
we sit together on the slab
You stare into mine
a mesmerizing feeling when
the girl that you love
returns your stare into oblivion
lost on the wakes of bliss.

The bedframe shatters like a destroyed mirror
        beneath our joint weight
the mattress deflates
I mount her
she pulls me down

My words come out in short bursts of static
like a whale resurfacing for air
        an excited flirtation device
        when our faces lock together
                for the rest of the night.
The surging pleasure
overtakes my soul
                I have arrived

        at the end of the line....

The TR*TH

Introducing "The TR*TH"

I'm sober, I'm happy------but I'm lonely, and at times I feel so utterly drab as if all hope is depleting me, and soon I'll be stuck in a nihilistic sea of angst and frustration....

But don't get me wrong, I like being sober, I like this life, I like being here, and if I wasn't me, but someone else, I'd be even worse off, I suppose.

So all this bitching and moaning from me is just what I have to do to vent at times, to let out my frustration so that it doesn't burrow deep inside me and bob its head out at the worst possible moment---

and you all know what would happen then, right?

Part 1

The world
me
I sit in unisons and
I feel the hate coming through
the door------I sit here
bored and feeling
mischievous, menacing glares
------I'm BORED!
How many times must
I tell you?
I'm racking my fists
against the door,
my skin blistering beneath
the reverberating pelts/

I sit in the room
and it's silent
and still
      and I wanna go out
      and I wanna live my life
but I have no life
to live....

My friends come and go
bustling one moment
dissipating the next....

I have a few friends
but they have no names....
They're nameless entities
soulless demons
who will eat you
for dinner
       yum yum yum!

The music plays fast
I got a headache
      I Want It Faster
or the pain in my head
will never settle....
      PLAY IT LOUDER

You don't know
You will never know
You stuff yourself with
Facebook and YouTube
and boring distractions alike

but you don't know me....

I'm alone
I'm alone
I sit in a dark shadow waiting
I wait forever and no one ever comes
along and saves me....
I had girlfriends but they hate me/
so what's the point? if I'm
not getting laid today.

I JUST GOT
BETTER THINGS TO DO!!!

A man told me what girls want.
Girls want what girls want, he said.

I refuse to play your silly games---
I JUST GOT
BETTER THINGS TO DO!!!

Although it would be nice
---WUD BE?---
if I had me a slave
a slave who would spread
her legs on command and let
me stick it in whenever I wanted
to.

Guess I'm lonely---
that's just a terminal
reality for me, but

I JUST GOT
BETTER THINGS TO DO!!!

Your life
Your hell
Your World

is not right for me.

I lived in the gutter
with other junkies and
scumfucs alike,
dirty and drugged out---
but today things are
different:

For one,
        I'M SOBER
cuz

I JUST GOT
BETTER THINGS TO DO!!!

I was a lowlife boozer
way back when
but today I'm a
changed man, a scholarly man
an author, but still on the lowdown
which in turn makes me a
lowlife scholar, I suppose
a literate lowlife
a lowlife higher than life
higher than you ...

but I JUST GOT
BETTER THINGS TO DO!!!

Part 2

This is where the
trouble starts it starts with
cliques clubs posses or whatever///
It starts when unions are
formed, that's why I hate
PUNK ROCK
slimy cunts, all of them....

You think you're cool,
with your trendy badges
You Trendy Fucks
with your spikey, died hair
your painted black leather jackets,
you colors and your slogans
and your preaching bullshit------
Last I checked, school
is not in session---so save
your preaching for someone
who gives a shit---cuz I couldn't
care less:
How much did that jacket
cost you?
            anyway

NO

I'm me, I'm no Punk
I'm me, I'm just a runt....
I'm me me me! and searching
endlessly for fun.

I JUST GOT
BETTER THINGS TO DO!!!

So I sit here going nowhere
wishing for things
just out of reach
if only they'd come a little
closer
I would be put at ease,
but it's not that easy

NEVER WAS-----------

Part 3

THE HEADLINES read
      another man
      dead
      another child
      abducted
      another young girl
      raped & beaten---
this I know---

I don't need the damn TV
to tell me this
the newspaper to spell it
out for me---

this I know....

PERIOD

The world is in crisis
<u>STOP</u>
the terrorists have won
<u>STOP</u>
DRUGS & GUNS and prostitution
rule supreme and there's
no point in fighting it …
anymore

<u>STOP STOP STOP</u>

This is RUTLAND
home of the junkie
You think your life
is in a rut?
Wait till you're
taking it up the butt by
robbers
and corrupt cops
and high-&-mighty pseudo-
hippies who think their
way is right------

I JUST GOT
BETTER THINGS TO DO!!!

In <u>this</u> world
      run by
      Facebook, run by social media
      and the like, the <u>real</u> media
      needs a way in, an avenue so
      they can continue to rape us
      with their rhetorical rubbish
so they can continue to
own our souls.

THIS IS WHAT AMERICA
is doing to you, but
today
in <u>this</u> world
      run by
      Facebook, run by social media
      and the like, the <u>real</u> media
      needs a way in, an avenue so
      they can continue to rape us
      with their rhetorical rubbish

I JUST GOT
BETTER THINGS TO DO!!!

I'd much rather read
a book, write a poem,
learn something new, explore
a new idea---cuz a guy says to me

Saturday night he says:
Knowledge is power....

But
today
in this world
        run by
        Facebook, run by social media
        and the like, the real media
        needs a way in, an avenue so
        they can continue to rape us
        with their rhetorical rubbish
do they really?

Knowledge might be power
but money is godliness
stupidity is royalty ...

and I'm smart in an age
that values dumb dumb dumb
people---what's next?
        To be rewarded for slapping your
        chest one too many times.
        To be rewarded for
        biting your own ear off....

If you pay me, I might just
leap off a roof and plunge right
into a bush---

wouldn't be the first time
I've done
such a thing.
How much money would you give me
to see me slam my head
into a brick wall?...

I was doing that for free
and now I've found that people
will actually pay good money
to see that....

Start a YouTube channel,
film me screaming at a hamburger---
bound to make millions, you know....

Part 4

I'm a hopeless romantic
on the run from
myself, tied up to one
girl
and then another
all for
      what?

It's going nowhere....
I lived that way
for way too long
don't you see
Girls for girls
surfing the hot waves
of pink pleasure
all for
      what?

It's an endless struggle
this mindless hope
roping me in like barbed wire
I'm tangled
I'm cut
stuck in a tangle of needles
all for
      what?

I'm a nihilist
I believe in NOthing
but then there's something
out there beyond me
There has to be, and I pray to
it
what is it?
A Dream, A Scheme, it's got me
tied to the magazines
of love
This love

I JUST GOT
BETTER THINGS TO DO!!!

I run for cover
lurking beneath railroad bridges
with other freaks like me------
They drink their 40s
I drink my caffeine
We scream and we
shout for something
or another
        something more
        something better
We want it all

The TV promised a good life
The movies promised a
happy ending, but in this life
nothing ever ends------
It just goes on and on
swirling into madness
THIS is my madness
THIS is me
    here
        now
The only ending I know of

is in the back of a black
hearse
your body burned to ashes
and the ashes
        packed into the bottom of
a yearn
        and hurled off the bridge
        into icy waters

That's not the way I want to
go---
I do want a happy ending though
I do want some relief
but all I've got is a hand
to rub myself with as the white tears
spurt out of me
like smoke>>>>>>>>>>>>>>

I'm sad
sick of being here....

I'm alone and the
world is trying to censor me
THE TITLE OF this POEM
is "The TR*TH," for this is my
TRUTH, uncensored
unabashed
unrestricted
        there's too much
        friction in this world
        too many
        restrictions trying to hold us
down

and I'm plummeting
down
down

down

I JUST GOT
BETTER THINGS TO DO!!!

I'm sober now
don't you see?
I'm living the nightmare
but at least I'm
sober now........................

It
could
always
be
worse, I remind myself
when the shit hits the fan
when the riots start

and we have to run for cover

THIS IS AMERICA, my friend
and as such I want my rights///

I Want the Right to Be ME
That's the TRUTH
of it..............................

Part 5

The AMERICAN DREAM
      or moreover
      the AMERICAN NIGHTMARE
      for me....

I lived in the
AMERICAN DREAM
in Newton, Massachusetts
where you can be a star
or just a loser
      I was a LOSER
that's my AMERICAN DREAM
it wasn't pretty------
I got cornered in the locker room
after gym class where STARS
surrounded me and one
put me in a chokehold
and smashed my head
into the concrete floor

The AMERICAN DREAM
      or moreover
      the AMERICAN NIGHTMARE
      for me....

I got cornered at the Store 24

and beaten with an inch of my life
as the guy threatened to kill me
        for what?
        for looking different than him?

I'd take my chances in Dorchester
in Mattapan
on Blue Hills Ave., with the bloods
and crypts, at war selling drugs
& guns
and prostitutes///

I've been to the inner city
a place where kids from my
hometown should not roam
ever
        It's not safe
        for whom?
        Who are you trying
        to protect?

I've always felt safer there
than I ever did in
Newton<<< Home of the
AMERICAN DREAM.
The American Dream was a myth
and these black kids of
the ghetto had the right idea
by exploiting it
with drugs
& guns
and prostitutes---get your suckysucky
fuckyfucky
on while you're at it.

They had a vision
They had accepted it as such
They had come to realize that

the AMERICAN DREAM had no place
for them, and so
        they lived on the skids///

I JUST GOT
BETTER THINGS TO DO!!!

Every day I see some hot chick
dressed in her skintight clothing
to show off her tits and ass
and maybe even a camel toe
        in search of
        the AMERICAN DREAM

to find a sugar daddy
to spread the wealth>>>>

I haven't had a <u>real</u> dream
in years
only nightmares stream thru my mind
at night
when I sleep
because the things that I seeked
and dreamed of
all my life
i discovered later on
to be ridden with filth

I was disillusioned
My prior illusion of
        the AMERICAN DREAM
was smashed
stuffed in a blender, and I
saw a side of life most people
never see cuz they're too busy
accepting the lie

Hey, the lie accepts them

so why not?

But me
I saw past the lie
I had no choice
It was either that or
      get trampled by
      white men dawning blue
      suits and brandishing
      blue briefcases filled with
      paperwork//

I JUST GOT
BETTER THINGS TO DO!!!

The AMERICAN DREAM
is not what it seems
The American Dream
is just not for me///

When I dream about AMERICA
the only thing I see
is red, and it fills my vision
like spilt blood
      ------that's my American dream)))